"Jews in America"; Re-print by Courtesy of Funk & Wagnalls Company From Vol. I., Pages 492 to 505 of the Jewish Encyclopedia..

E 184
.J5 A2
Copy 1

"Jews in America"

Re-print by courtesy of Funk & Wagnalls Company *from* Vol. I., pages 492 to 505 *of the* Jewish Encyclopedia

Cyrus Adler

Copyright entered according to act of Congress in the year 1901, by
FUNK & WAGNALLS COMPANY
NEW YORK AND LONDON

E184
.J5A2

228181*

JEWS IN AMERICA.

[Being a Reprint of the Article "America" from Volume I. of The Jewish Encyclopedia, Written by Dr Cyrus Adler, Assistant Secretary of the Smithsonian Institution, Washington, D. C.]

AMERICA: The name "America" is used in this article in its broadest signification, as applied to the entire western world, that is, North and South America and all the adjacent islands

The discovery of America by Columbus, and the earliest expeditions and attempts at settlement in various parts of the continent and in many of the contiguous islands, are intimately connected with the Jews and their history

Columbus received great assistance from astronomical works prepared by Jews, and from scientific instruments of which Jews were the inventors Luis de Santangel and Gabriel Sanchez—both Maranos—and Juan Cabrero, of Jewish descent, urged upon Queen Isabella the importance of the plans of Columbus, and were instrumental in securing the funds for the first and second voyages The expenses of the latter were defrayed almost exclusively out of moneys derived from the confiscated properties of Jews

Jews Accompany Columbus.

At least five persons of Jewish blood accompanied Columbus upon his first voyage, among whom special mention must be made of Luis de Torres, who was to have acted in the capacity of interpreter Torres is said to have been the first European to tread the soil of America, and the first to discover the use of tobacco He settled and died in Cuba

On March 31, 1492, the Catholic monarchs issued a decree to the effect that within four months all Jews and Jewesses were to leave the kingdoms and lands of Spain On April 30 the decree was publicly announced by the heralds, and on the same day Columbus was ordered to equip a fleet for his voyage to the Indies On Aug 2, 1492, about 300,000 Jews left Spain to settle wherever they might find a shelter, and on the following day the fleet of Columbus set sail His journal opens with a reference to the coincidence in time of these two events Columbus' first account of his discovery took the form of a letter to his Jewish patron, Santangel

The facts mentioned suffice to explain the very early presence of Jews in America (see Kayserling, "Christopher Columbus and the Participation of Jews in the Spanish and Portuguese Discoveries," New York, 1894, and the article AMERICA, DISCOVERY OF, JEW ENCY Vol I)

Brazil · Brazil was discovered in 1499 by a Spaniard, Pinzon, and independently in 1500 by a Portuguese, Pedro Alvarez de Cabral With him was a

Jewish mariner, Gaspar, who was of much assistance in the discovery of Brazil and who is favorably mentioned by Amerigo Vespucci (Kayserling, *l.c.* p. 117). Brazil was the part of America earliest inhabited by large numbers of Jews. Portugal sent annually two shiploads of Jews, and criminals, and also deported persons who had been condemned by the Inquisition. The Maranos are said

Early Portuguese Colonies. to have quickly thrown off their mask and to have professed Judaism. As early as 1548 (according to some, 1531) Portuguese Jews, it is asserted, transplanted the sugar-cane from Madeira to Brazil; but whether this be true or false, it is indisputable that nearly all the large sugar-plantations of Brazil during the first half of the seventeenth century belonged to Jews.

So extensive had the emigration to Portuguese colonies become in 1557 that on June 30 of that year an edict was issued forbidding Maranos to leave Portugal. A stringent law was passed prohibiting the settlement of Jews in the Spanish colonies as well, yet some of position and wealth were among the early settlers. This is indicated by the fact that the prohibition was removed in 1577 upon the payment by the Jews in the colonies of the enormous sum of 1,700,000 cruzados, equivalent to about $714,000. In 1611 mention is made of wealthy Maranos making the return trip from Bahia to Portugal.

That Jews had settled in Brazil, prior to the Dutch occupation, in sufficient numbers to make them a military factor, is shown by the argument advanced in favor of an attack by the Dutch West India Company on the Portuguese in Brazil, "that the Jews there would be ready to aid the Dutch in any attempt." This attack was successfully made in 1624, at which time all the Jews in the country united in the formation of a congregation. Jews had invested largely in the Dutch

Under Dutch Rule. West India Company; and to this fact the favorable attitude of the Holland authorities is traceable. Those who had come over under Portuguese and Dutch rule were reenforced in 1642 by a party of 600 from Amsterdam, bringing with them Ḥakam Isaac Aboab, who settled at Recife (Pernambuco), and was probably the first rabbi in Brazil. Among these settlers was also Ephraim Sueiro, a step-brother of Manasseh ben Israel. Manasseh himself intended to emigrate to Brazil, as is learned from a letter of Vossius to Grotius; but he was dissuaded by the leading men of his community. There were also settlements at Parahiba, Bahia, and Rio de Janeiro. It is estimated that at Recife alone there were more than 5,000 Jews in 1654.

The Brazilian Jews enjoyed the same rights as other Dutch subjects; and they rendered valuable services both as soldiers and in civil life.

The first Spanish and Portuguese settlers in America, other than banished criminals, were adventurers seeking land for the crown or gold for themselves. This was not true of the Jews. Expelled first from Spain, next from Portugal, they desired only a place in which they might have the opportunity to live and to throw off the mask of Christianity which they had been forced to wear. Though they engaged largely in commerce—in which they had especial advantages, having correspondents in Venice, in Turkey, and in other countries to which their coreligionists had emigrated—they counted among their number several scholars, and during the Dutch occupation maintained friendly relations with learned men in Amsterdam.

The first trace of Jewish literature in America is found in 1636, when some Brazilian Jews, in dispute about liturgical questions, sought counsel of Rabbi Hayyim Shabbethai of Salonica. In the middle of the seventeenth century there were living in Brazil, in addition to Rabbi Isaac Aboab mentioned above,

First American Jewish Scholar. a well-known Talmudist, Jacob Lagarto, and the poet ELIYAHU MACHORRO. Apparently the first Jewish scholar born on American soil was JACOB DE VELOSINO, born in Pernambuco in 1657, a philosopher, physician, and polemical writer of ability.

In 1646 war broke out between the Dutch and the Portuguese; and in this struggle, which lasted nine years, the Jews aided the Dutch until the end. The Dutch capitulation (1654) contained a rather ominous clause wherein the Portuguese promised to the Jews "an amnesty in all wherein they could promise it." The sufferings of the Jews in this war are related in a poem by Isaac Aboab, which is probably the earliest product extant of Jewish authorship on American soil.

Although it does not appear that the Inquisition was formally established in Brazil, there is evidence to the effect that the Holy Office seized suspected persons and sent them to Portugal for trial. At all events, the Portuguese conquest was followed by the dispersion of the Jewish colony. Many returned to Amsterdam, some went to the French settlements—Guadeloupe, Martinique, and Cayenne—some to Curaçao, and others to New Amsterdam. We have travelers' statements to the effect that as late as 1850 a few remained in Brazil as Maranos; and in very recent times small congregations have been formed.

Mexico: Mexico, which contained the most highly civilized aborigines on the American continent, was invaded by Cortez in 1519; the capital was captured in 1521, and the country made a Spanish colony under the name of Nueva España (New Spain).

The most authentic information concerning the Jews of Mexico is unhappily contained in the records of the Inquisition, from which accurate, if not detailed, accounts are derived.

The first auto da fé celebrated in New Spain was held in the year 1536; and the first Jew, or rather "Judaizer" (*Judaisant*), as he was called, mentioned in these records is a certain Francisco Millan, who was "reconciled" in the year 1539. His case seems, however, to have been a solitary one; since for many years after all of those tried by the Inquisition were Lutherans or persons otherwise suspected of heresy.

In 1571 the Inquisition was formally established in Mexico, for the purpose "of freeing the land,

Jews and the Inquisition. which had been contaminated by Jews and heretics, especially of the Portuguese nation." It is not until 1578 that the names of Jews—three in that year—are again met with; and from that time on, until the close of the Inquisition records of Mexico in 1803 (the Holy Office was not formally disestablished in Mexico until 1820), a large proportion, possibly as many as one-half, of those tried were Jews. Since all of these were Maranos, and a great number of the secret Jews must have escaped the eye of the Inquisition, a fair conception may thus be obtained of the very considerable number who settled and lived in Mexico during this period. Paramus, the historian, writing in 1599, states that in spite of all obstacles the Jews publicly celebrated their Passover; but the statement is open to question.

Some idea of the number of Jews in Mexico in the middle of the seventeenth century may be gained from the fact that, in a single trial by the Inquisition—that of a boy in 1642—the names of no less than eighty-six Judaizers are mentioned. It is generally assumed that one of the principal motives of the Inquisition was the confiscation of estates; and it is unquestionably true that a considerable proportion of the Jews tried in Mexico were mine-owners or merchants. Nevertheless, there must have been many Mexican Jews in the humbler walks of life. Between 1600 and 1650 the following occupations of Jews and Jewesses are recorded: butcher, gilder, baker, sugar-hawker, peanut-vender, silversmith, juggler, nurserymaid, and seamstress.

In recent times Jews have again immigrated to Mexico; and for a short time a Jewish journal was published in the capital city.

From 1590 until the revolt of Mexico from Spanish rule the Philippine Islands were governed through the viceroy and audiencia of Mexico; and prior to 1601 at least four Jews had gone from Mexico to the city of Manila.

Other South American States: Peru was captured by the Spanish in 1533-34; and many Spanish Jews took refuge in Lima. Philip II. took rigorous measures against them, and early introduced the Inquisition. From imperfect records it appears that a Jew was burnt there in 1581. In 1639 twelve Portuguese merchants, supposed to be Jews, were burnt, one of them being described as "the Judaizing millionaire Manuel Bautista Perez." Six thousand Portuguese, of whom it may be assumed many were Jews, purchased the right of residence upon the payment of 200,000 ducats. It appears to be the opinion of writers upon the Inquisition that in Lima the Holy Office was particularly rapacious, and that all rich Portuguese were charged with being Judaizers. Yet it is extremely likely that this cynical view is incorrect, and that the larger number of Portuguese in Peru in early **Peru.** days were actually Maranos. A few details of the history of the Jews in Peru are known, through a memoir composed from original manuscript sources by B. Vicuna MacKenna, of a certain Francisco Moyen, who suffered most grievously from the Inquisition in the eighteenth century. In very recent times Jews to the number of about 500 have resettled in Peru.

Jews are also to be found in very small numbers in Venezuela, Costa Rica, and other South American states. To the Argentine Republic, however, there has been a systematic immigration, due directly to the efforts of Baron de Hirsch. It is estimated that there are now settled in that country about 6,755 Jews (see AGRICULTURAL COLONIES IN THE ARGENTINE REPUBLIC).

Surinam: As early as 1644 the Jews commenced to go in small numbers to Paramaribo. In 1662 Lord Willoughby secured from Charles II. permission to colonize Surinam; and two years later the Jewish colony of Cayenne, which had been disbanded, removed to Surinam.

In February, 1667, Surinam, then an English colony, surrendered to a Dutch fleet. The articles of surrender provided that English subjects disposed to leave the colony should be at liberty to do so. Six months later Surinam was retaken by the English fleet and became again an English colony; but by the treaty of Breda (July 16, 1667) it was restored to the Dutch. The circumstance became important because the British government made strong representations to Holland on behalf of Jewish residents of Surinam who, under this clause of the treaty, desired to leave for Jamaica, but to whom the Dutch authorities at Surinam refused permission to depart, on account of their wealth and standing. In spite of the "alien" status of Jews domiciled in English possessions from the point of view of British law, the Council of Great Britain found it expedient to recognize Jews as British subjects at this early date.

The Dutch continued to the Jews the **Jews** privileges which had been accorded **Regarded** them by the English. A synagogue **as British** was built at Savanna, which was **Subjects.** called "Jews' Town," and is said to have been inhabited exclusively by Jews. Another and a larger synagogue was erected at Paramaribo.

Many of the colonists—probably the major part of them—left with the English fleet under Captain Willoughby, and settled in Jamaica and Barbados. In 1669 the Dutch government gave the Jews of Surinam a formal promise that they would be allowed the free exercise of their religion. They were largely engaged in agriculture, and were the first cultivators of the sugar-cane in Surinam. When, in 1689, a French fleet made a sudden attack upon Surinam it was met with brave resistance by the Jews, under Samuel Nassy; and on a second attack in 1712, the Jews, under Captain Isaac Pinto, made a stubborn fight. They were also foremost in the suppression of the negro revolts from 1690 to 1772. The first rabbi in Surinam was Isaac Neto: the date of his immigration to the colony must have been about 1674.

In 1685 the Congregation Berakah we-Shalom of Savanna built a splendid synagogue. This was probably rendered possible by the considerable additions to the colony from Brazil after the reconquest of the country by the Portuguese. In 1890 the Jews in Surinam numbered about 1,560, having two synagogues, one following the Spanish and the other the German rite.

Cayenne: A colony was established here probably as early as 1650; and this was augmented by a party of 152 which set sail for Cayenne in August, 1660. Among them was the Spanish-Jewish poet, historian, and litterateur Miguel (or Daniel) de Barrios. In 1664 the colony at Cayenne was dissolved; the inhabitants moving to Surinam (as stated above), to Jamaica, and to Barbados.

Curaçao: In 1650 twelve Jewish families were brought to Curaçao.

In 1652 two leagues of land along the coast for fifty families, and four leagues for one hundred families, were granted by the Dutch West India Company to Joseph Nuñez de Fonseca (alias David Nassi) and others, to found a colony of Jews in that island. As early as 1654, direct relations between these settlers and the inhabitants of New Netherlands were established. In that year immigrants of wealth and standing arrived in considerable numbers from Brazil. The first burial-ground was established in 1656; and by 1692 the Congregation Mikveh Israel had completed its synagogue. A second congregation, Neveh Shalom, was established in 1740, and in 1865 a Reform congregation, under the name "Emanuel." In 1690 a party of about ninety set sail for North America, and established themselves in Rhode Island (Newport).

West Indies: In 1502 King Ferdinand prohibited the settlement in the West Indies of any more Jews; and in 1506 he ordered the bishops to proceed against such as might be already settled there. As noted above, Luis de Torres, who accompanied Columbus on his first voyage, settled and died in Cuba. It is asserted that as early as 1493 young Jewish children were, after baptism, sent to the island of St. Thomas. In 1642 mention is made of a certain Miguel Nuñez, a Marano in Cuba; and some authorities incline to the opinion that the first considerable settlement of Jews in New Amsterdam came from that island.

Barbados: Jews settled in Barbados as early as 1628; but the first definite information relates to the year 1661, when certain traders petitioned the king to permit them to live and trade in Barbados and Surinam. As early as 1664 reference is made to a Jew, named Señor Abraham Israel de Pisa, who found gold in the island. Another person of nearly the same name, Isaac Israel de Piso, fell under the king's displeasure in March, 1665, owing to his failure to find the expected gold-mines. In 1668 Jews are mentioned as owners of sugar-works. In 1671 Moses Pereyra was made a free denizen; and in 1673 the Jews began an agitation for recognition of their rights as citizens. On Feb. 18, 1674,

Privileges as to Taking Oath. a law was passed granting them the privilege of taking the oath upon the five books of Moses; and in January, 1675, a favorable response was made by the Assembly to their petition for the extension of their trade privileges. In 1676 Governor Sir Jonathan Atkins reported that there were about 30 Jewish families of Dutch extraction from Brazil. On Oct. 29, 1679, Jacob Senior arrived at Barbados. In the year 1680, according to a contemporary document, there were 54 adult Jews and 182 children, residing in and about the town of St. Michaels. These Jews owned a large number of slaves. In 1679 a few of the Barbados Jews emigrated—3 to London, 2 to Jamaica, and 1 to Surinam. According to the census of 1891 there were 21 Jewish families on the island.

Jamaica: Jews probably settled here in considerable numbers in the second half of the sixteenth century.

The first Jews—six in number—who were introduced into Jamaica under British government in 1663, came on the ship "Great Guest," Captain Bernard. In December, 1671, Governor Lynch reported to Lord Arlington that the king could have no more profitable subjects than the Jews. Meanwhile petitions of merchants against them were considered by the king's council; the request being that the Jews be restricted to wholesale trade, which proposition the council rejected. In 1700 the Jews presented to Sir William Beeston, governor-in-chief of Jamaica, a petition asking for exemption from special taxes, and reciting other grievances.

The trade between London and Jamaica was principally in Jewish hands; and by 1750 about 200 Jews resided and had been naturalized in that island. One of the best-known literary men of Jamaica was Daniel Israel Lopez, who translated the Psalms into Spanish. At the present day there is a flourishing Jewish community in Jamaica.

Leeward Islands: On Aug. 31, 1694, an act was passed to prevent Jews from engrossing commodities imported into the Leeward Islands, which act was repealed in 1701—an indication that there must have been an early settlement of considerable proportions there.

Porto Rico: Of Porto Rico nothing is known concerning any early Jewish settlement. In recent years, since the Spanish-American war, Jews have immigrated thither; and there is now a flourishing congregation.

The Resettlement in England and Its Relation to America: Not without great interest is the intimate connection between American history and the resettlement of Jews in England. According to Lucien Wolf, "American history really played a very considerable part in bringing about the return of the Jews to England." It was in America that religious liberty won its first victory. A Jewish traveler, Antonio de Montezinos, was fully persuaded that in the American Indians he had found the Lost Ten Tribes—a belief which has had an extraordinary vitality. He related this story to Manasseh ben Israel; and his narrative made a profound impression. This fact accorded with

Aborigines and Lost Ten Tribes. the view of the times, that the dispersion was complete except for one particular land, England; and Manasseh argued that if the Jews would return to England, the Messiah would come. This view he promulgated in his work, "The Hope of Israel." The notion that the American aborigines were the Lost Ten Tribes has played an important part among Americanists. Besides those named above, it was held by Roldan, Garcia, Thorowgood, Adair, and Lord Kingsborough; and, though without important adherents among students of the American aborigines, it is still discussed as a theory to be considered.

It seems not unlikely that some of the members of the Crypto-Jewish community in London, prior to the Restoration, came from the American continent.

United States: The greatest prosperity and the largest population reached by any nation on the American continent have been attained by the United States; it is not surprising, therefore, that it now contains a larger number of Jews than any country in the world save Russia and Austria.

About forty years after the settlement of New Amsterdam Jews commenced to arrive there. They gradually made their way to all of the original thirteen colonies; and by the time of the outbreak of the Revolutionary War, they had in several communities reached honorable positions in commerce and in society.

Most of the early colonists in North America were of Sephardic stock, and came from Brazil, West Indies, Portugal, and Holland. At a

Early Colonists Mainly Sephardic. later date some came from England. Yet German and Polish Jews came to America much earlier than is usually supposed. Some of these settled in Pennsylvania, New York, Maryland, Virginia, and South Carolina in the earliest Colonial period. The Sephardim, however—at this time constituting the larger number—usually organized the congregations; and the fact of the early immigration of Ashkenazic Jews has thus been lost sight of by most writers. German Jews seem even to have been among the martyrs of the Inquisition in Mexico.

New York: By a letter written April 4, 1652, from Amsterdam by the director of the West India Company to the governor and council of New Netherlands, it appears that Jews were on the muster-rolls of soldiers and sailors sent out to the colony, and that they engaged to serve for a term of one year. As early as 1655 there were both Portuguese and German Jews in the colony.

The first Jewish settler in New Amsterdam whose name has been handed down was Jacob Barsimson,

First Jewish Settlers. who arrived on July 8, 1654, in the ship "Pear Tree." He was followed in the same year by a party of 23, who arrived in the bark "St. Catarina." It is generally assumed that they came from Brazil, although it is also held that they started from some part of the West Indies, most likely Cuba; and some had, unquestionably, spent a longer or a shorter time in Jamaica. They were received in an unfriendly fashion by Stuyvesant, the Dutch governor of New Amsterdam, who wrote to the directors of the Dutch West India Company asking authority for their exclusion. This the directors refused to grant (April 26, 1655) on the ground of "the considerable loss sustained by the Jews in the taking of Brazil, and also because of the large amount of capital which they have invested in the shares of the company." They directed that "they [the Jews] shall have permission to sail to and trade in New Netherland, and to live and remain there." This permission was modified on March 13, 1656, by the statement that the Jews were not privileged to erect a synagogue; and a little later they were precluded from employment in any public service, and from opening retail shops.

Early Privileges and Restrictions.

One of the sturdiest pioneers of the New Amsterdam colony was Asser Levy. In 1655 he, among others, applied to be enlisted in the militia; but permission was refused, and, in common with all other Jews, he was, instead, ordered to pay a tax. This he refused to do; and on Nov. 5, 1655, he petitioned for leave to stand guard like other burghers of New Amsterdam. The petition was rejected; but Levy seems to have appealed to Holland, for it subsequently appears that he was permitted to do guardduty like other citizens. Step by step, through the courts and by appeals, he secured many other privileges (see NEW YORK and ASSER LEVY). He seems to have been the first Jew in the state of New York to hold real estate: a lot on what is now the site of Albany was owned by him in 1661.

Another of the most prominent of the early Jews in New Amsterdam was Abraham de Lucena, who in 1655 applied, with several others, for permission to purchase a site for a burial-ground. The request was refused with the statement that there was then no need for it. On July 14, 1656, however, the request was granted.

New Amsterdam was captured by the British in 1664 and its name changed to New York. For a half-century afterward but little is known respecting the Jewish residents. Their increase in numbers was very moderate. It seems likely that they had some sort of private worship very soon after 1655, and that they began to meet in a more or less public way in 1673. In 1682 the congregation rented a house on Mill street; and it was not until 1729 that this was exchanged for a regular synagogue building.

On Nov. 15, 1727, an act was passed by the General Assembly of New York providing that when the oath of abjuration was to be taken by any one of his British Majesty's subjects professing the Jewish religion, the words "upon the true faith of a Christian" might be omitted. Three days later an act was passed naturalizing one Daniel Nunez da Costa.

Under British Rule.

There was a very considerable antipathy in the colony both to Catholics and to Jews; but in the case of the latter this gradually relaxed, so that they soon came to receive most of the privileges accorded to other inhabitants of the town and province. In 1737, however, the Assembly of New York decided that no Jew might vote for a member of that body.

Before and during the Revolutionary War the Jews, like the other inhabitants of New York, were divided in their allegiance. Many were devoted to the patriot cause; and among these was the minister of the congregation, Gershom Mendes Seixas, who, upon the occupation of New York by the British, took all the belongings of the synagogue and, with quite a number of the members, removed to Philadelphia, where he founded the first regularly established congregation, the Mickve Israel. After the close of the war most of these Jews returned to New York, which, on the decline of Newport as a commercial city, took its place and rapidly attracted a large population. The tide of immigration now commenced to flow toward the United States, most largely in the first instance to New York city. Hither came Jews from the West Indies, from Germany, Poland, Russia, Rumania, in short, from every quarter of the globe. It is estimated that the city of New York alone now (1901) contains 500,000 Jews; and there are 110 congregations enumerated exclusive of numerous small ones. Jews are now represented in New York city in every walk of life, professional, commercial, and industrial.

Modern Jewry of New York.

From the city, Jews gradually penetrated into the state. A congregation was founded at Buffalo in 1835, one at Albany in 1837, and another at Rochester in 1848; and all of the larger and many of the smaller towns in New York state now have Jewish communities.

Newport, R. I.: The hostile attitude of Stuyvesant probably caused Jewish emigrants to leave New Amsterdam as early as 1655 and to settle in Newport. There is definite information to the effect that 15 Jewish families arrived in 1658, who brought with them the first degrees of Masonry. They were reinforced by a contingent from Curaçao in 1690.

Quite in contrast with the oppressive treatment in New Amsterdam was the generous reception accorded the Jews in Rhode Island, in consonance with the liberal principles propounded by Roger Williams. Already in the seventeenth century the Jews of Newport had commercial relations with their coreligionists in New Amsterdam.

Jews Cordially Received.

It is likely that religious services were first held in Newport in 1658, although no synagogue was erected until the following century. A burial-place, however, was purchased on Feb. 28, 1677.

In 1750 a very important accession was received in the families of Lopez, Rivera, Pollock, Hart, and Hays, all persons of wealth and enterprise engaged in manufacture and commerce. These families came from Spain, Portugal, and the West Indies. The extent of the property of Aaron Lopez is shown by the fact that at one time he owned as many as 30 vessels. Jacob Rodrigues-Rivera, a native of Portugal, came to Newport about 1745. He was the first person to introduce the manufacture of spermaceti in America.

In 1762 the erection of a synagogue was begun, which was completed and dedicated in the following year. Two years previously there had come from Jamaica the Rev. Isaac Touro, who was chosen rabbi; and under his auspices the synagogue was well attended until the outbreak of the American Revolution. In 1763 there were between 60 and 70 Jewish families in Newport. The first Jewish sermon preached in America which has been published was delivered in the Newport synagogue on May 28, 1773, by Rabbi Ḥayyim Isaac Karigel, in the Spanish language, and was afterward translated into English. Karigel appears to have come from Hebron in Palestine, and was a close friend of Ezra Stiles, the president of Yale University. As early as 1761 a Jewish club was formed, with a membership limited to 9 persons. Just before the outbreak of the Revolutionary War the Jewish population of Newport

Synagogue Built.

appears to have comprised about 200 families. The community was dispersed by the war; and it never regained its importance. In 1790 it presented an address to Washington. The Touro family bequeathed sufficient money to maintain the synagogue as well as the cemetery; and these are still in existence, although the number of Jews now resident in Newport is but small.

The Jewish community of Newport held an especially interesting and even a unique position in America, and impressed itself for all time on the town, once the leading port of the colonies and now the most fashionable summer resort in the United States.

Other Parts of New England: An occasional Jew may have strayed into other portions of New England in the early days; but the Puritan atmosphere was apparently not congenial. The best known of the early settlers was Judah Monis, who became a convert to Christianity, and filled the chair of Hebrew in Harvard College from 1722 until his death in 1764.

As early as 1670 there is mention of a Jew, Jacob Lucene, in the Colonial Records of Connecticut.

When the British took Newport many of the Jews there left and effected a temporary settlement at Leicester, Mass.; but this did not survive the close of the war. A number of Jews, including the Hays family, settled at Boston before 1800. About 1840 Jews began to emigrate from New York to New Haven and Boston; and congregations were formed in those cities in 1840 and 1842 respectively.

New Haven and Boston. The communal life of the New England Jews was without especial incident; and their numbers increased but slowly until after the beginning of the great Russian emigration in 1882. Immediately the overflow from New York, as well as the emigration through Canada, commenced to pour into New England. It is estimated that 60,000 Jews now (1901) reside in Massachusetts alone, and nearly 20,000 more in the other New England states.

An interesting phenomenon has been noticed in connection with the shifting of agricultural industry in the United States. With the opening up of the Western country and the greater advantages offered by the virgin soil, many New England farmers absolutely abandoned their comparatively unfruitful farms and moved West. These abandoned farms, especially in Connecticut, have been taken up by Russian Jews, who, principally as dairy farmers, have added a new and useful element to the agricultural community.

Russian Jews as Farmers.

Maryland: It seems not unlikely that Maryland was the first colony in which Jews settled, though they were probably stragglers; and it was long before any communal life was established.

Scattered Jews seem to have arrived shortly after the establishment of the provincial government in 1634. At least as early as 1657 Dr. Jacob Lumbrozo was settled there, and in 1658 he was tried and remanded for blasphemy, his release being due to the general amnesty in honor of the accession of Richard Cromwell (declared March 3, 1658). Letters of denization were issued to him Sept. 10, 1663. He had a plantation and also practised medicine. He is described as from Lisbon; but he had a sister in Holland.

The history of the Jews in Maryland is of especial interest; since it was in this colony and state that the civil and political rights of Jews were most restricted, and it was here, of all America, that the most systematic efforts were put forth for obtaining the fullest recognition under the law. Maryland was one of the first colonies to adopt religious toleration as the basis of the state; but it was toleration and not liberty, since there was a proviso that any person who denied the Trinity was to be punished with death. Even after the Revolution, no one might hold any office of profit or trust under the state without signing a declaration that he believed in the Christian religion.

Efforts were made in 1801 and 1804 to obtain a revocation of this proviso; but on both occasions more than two-thirds of the legislature voted against its repeal. These efforts were renewed in 1819, and finally succeeded, so that in 1824 two Jewish citizens were elected members of the Council of Baltimore, being the first Jews to hold office in the state of Maryland. The success of these efforts was largely due to the persistent labors of a single family—the Cohens—who still maintain an honored position in the community.

Jews Hold Public Positions.

At the outbreak of the Civil War, Maryland, although remaining in the Union, numbered among her citizens a large body of sympathizers with the Confederate cause. The conflict of opinion was especially severe among the Jews, due to the pronounced antislavery attitude assumed by Rabbi David Einhorn, who was actually threatened with violence and was obliged to leave the city.

Pennsylvania: Jews from New Amsterdam traded along South river, subsequently named the Delaware, as early as 1655, and began to arrive as settlers in the colony of Pennsylvania not much more than ten years after its establishment. Unlike New York and Newport, a very considerable proportion of the early Pennsylvania colonists were not Portuguese, but German Jews; and they settled not in Philadelphia, but in towns in the interior of the state. The earliest settlements seem to have been in Schaefersville and Lancaster. Joseph Simon, who in the latter place was the pioneer, about 1740 embarked in the Indian trade and in real-estate transactions on a large scale. In 1747 the deed for a Jewish cemetery in Lancaster was made out in his name and in that of Isaac Nunes Ricus as trustees. Myer Hart was one of the founders of Easton in 1750. He was engaged in trade, and was there naturalized on Oct. 3, 1764. Aaron Levy settled in Northumberland county, Pa., about 1760, and was a large landowner. In 1786 he founded the town of AARONSBURG in Centre county.

Schaefersville, Lancaster, and Easton.

The Jewish community of Philadelphia was for a time the leading one in the United States, and was inferior in numbers only to that of New York. The first Jewish settler in Philadelphia of whom there is record was Jonas Aaron (1703), and the second was Arnold Bamberger (1726). As early as 1747 a number of persons who had joined together for the purpose of worship met for services in a small house in Sterling alley—afterward in Cherry alley—between Third and Fourth streets. They were mostly German and Polish Jews; and their differences as to the liturgy to be followed prevented at the time the formation of any regular congregation. When the British troops occupied New York during the Revolutionary War, the minister, Gershom Mendes Seixas, with a considerable portion of the New York congregation, came to Philadelphia, and, finding no regular services, they, with the help of the resident Jews, established one in accordance with the Portuguese rite. Seixas was the first minister. After him no man of importance held the position until Isaac Leeser, 1829. He was the leading

Philadelphia.

Jewish minister of his time; and not more than two or three others have left such an impress upon American-Jewish affairs as he. Minister, teacher, organizer, translator of the Bible, editor, and publisher, he was in every way indefatigable. Other prominent persons were the Phillips family, chief among them being Zalegman Phillips, Henry M. Phillips, the latter one of the leading lawyers of Philadelphia and a member of the Thirty-fifth Congress. There followed Leeser, as minister of the Mickve Israel Congregation, Sabato Morais, a native of Leghorn, Italy, who from 1851 until his death in 1897 was a leading figure in American-Jewish affairs. He first suggested the Jewish Theological Seminary in New York.

Notable Philadelphia Jews.

The first German congregation was the Rodeph Shalom, which received a charter on Aug. 12, 1802, but which no doubt had meetings at an earlier date. The most prominent of its rabbis was Marcus Jastrow; the best-known cantor, Jacob Frankel. The latter acted during the Civil War as chaplain of hospitals under the United States government. The first leading Reform minister installed in Philadelphia was rabbi Samuel Hirsch. Many other congregations have since been formed, more especially since 1882, when the Russian immigration brought large numbers to the city.

Philadelphia has always been prominent in educational matters. The first Jewish Sunday-school was organized there in 1838; the Hebrew Education Society, in 1848; and the Maimonides College, in 1867. The largest fund in the United States for higher Jewish education is that provided by a deed of gift from Hyman Gratz to the Mickve Israel Congregation in trust, from which Gratz College is supported. One of the most comprehensive of works relating to Jews of any single community in the United States is "The Jews of Philadelphia," by Henry Samuel Morais, published in Philadelphia in 1894. Philadelphia Jews have been prominent in many professions, in the fine arts, and in all the avenues of manufacture and commerce. Up to 1894 as many as 116 had been admitted to the bar; and the number has since been greatly increased. Three Jews served in Congress as representatives of the state.

Maimonides and Gratz Colleges.

Jews gradually made their way to the western part of the state, settling in large numbers in Pittsburg, which, after Philadelphia, is the next largest community in Pennsylvania. That of Wilkesbarre is notable for its numbers and for the high character of its members. Since the Russian immigration Jews have made their way to every part of the state; and there is scarcely a town of any size which is now without its community or congregation.

Georgia: In none of the colonies which afterward formed the United States did the Jews arrive in numbers so early after the establishment of the colony as in Georgia. On July 7, 1733, Oglethorpe, its founder and governor, had assembled the colonists, who had arrived one month previously, on the site of the present city of Savannah for the purpose of allotting to each settler his proportion of land. While the colonists were partaking of a public dinner, given at the close of the day's proceedings, there came up the Savannah river, from London, a vessel containing 40 Jewish emigrants. Their arrival was not expected; but on the whole they were kindly received. One of their number, Dr. Nunis, was especially valuable for his attention to the sick. The trustees in London were opposed to the settlement of the Jews; but Oglethorpe included the names of a half-dozen of them as grantors in a conveyance, executed Dec. 21, 1733, of town lots, gardens, and farms. These original settlers, all of whom names have been recorded, were the progenitors of families still in existence in various parts of the United States. The first male white child born in the state of Georgia was a Jew, Isaac Minis. Abraham de Lyon had prior to 1737 introduced the culture of grapes, he having been a winegrower in Portugal. By 1742 the number of Jews in Savannah was so diminished that the services in the synagogue had to be discontinued, three only of the original families remaining. A quarter of a century later several returned from Charleston.

Savannah.

In 1774 another congregation was started, which was gradually augmented until the outbreak of the American Revolution. Immediately after the close of the war many Jews returned to Savannah; and on July 7, 1786, they hired a dwelling-house for a place of worship. On Nov. 30, 1790, a charter for a congregation, under the name of "Mickve Israel of Savannah," was granted. The religious exercises of the congregation were conducted gratuitously by Dr. de la Motta; and in 1820, on the occasion of the consecration of the synagogue, he delivered an address which is still a document of the very greatest value to American-Jewish history. The synagogue was destroyed by fire in 1829, and was replaced by a substantial structure of brick.

Augusta was the next town in the state settled by Jews. The first arrival—about 1825—was one Florence accompanied by his wife. Other families followed in 1826 from Charleston. The first congregation, B'ne Israel, was organized in 1846. Atlanta, Columbus, and Macon have considerable communities; and a number of congregations are scattered throughout the state; but the community in Savannah is still the most important. At Atlanta there is a Home for Orphans, founded and managed by the Independent Order B'ne B'rith.

Augusta, Macon, etc.

South Carolina: As early as 1742 Jews left Savannah and settled in Charleston. A congregation was formed in 1750, and its members worshiped for seven years in a small wooden house in Union street, near Queen street. They purchased a burial-ground in 1757, and in 1781 a large building in Union street which was altered and prepared for a synagogue. In 1791, when the congregation was incorporated, it consisted of 51 families, numbering in all about 400 persons. Two years later these had increased so much that a new synagogue was erected at a cost of $20,000, which was completed in 1794. The community was augmented after the Revolution by a large number of Jews from New York, who settled in Charleston, and remained there till the commencement of the Civil War. Jews are now settled in small numbers throughout the state. The first Reform movement in any congregation in America was instituted in Charleston in 1825.

Charleston.

North Carolina: In 1808 an attempt was made to expel a member of the General Assembly of North Carolina because of his Jewish faith. In 1826 the number of Jewish settlers in the state was estimated at 400, which was considerably augmented after the emigration of 1848. The largest community at the present time (1901) is that of Wilmington.

Virginia and West Virginia: Stray Jewish settlers came to Virginia about 1658, some of whose names and transactions have been handed down. At least one Jewish soldier—possibly two—served in Virginia regiments under Washington in his expedition across the Alleghany mountains in 1754. It is likely that quite a number of Jews removed from Baltimore and other points in Maryland to Richmond at an early date. The Congregation Beth Shalom was formed in the latter place about the year 1791. The Richmond community has since grown to considerable proportions, as has also that of Norfolk. Congregations now exist in about 20 towns in the state, and in at least 4 towns in West Virginia.

Louisiana: Judah Touro came to New Orleans as early as 1801. The first interment in the Jewish cemetery of that city took place on June 28, 1828. The community there grew rapidly from 1848 on; and numbers of congregations and important charitable organizations were established. Similar progress is noticeable throughout the entire state, 19 towns now having Jewish communities.

Kentucky: The first person of undoubted Jewish blood to settle in Kentucky was a Mr. Salamon, of Philadelphia, who established himself at Harrodsburg about 1808. In 1816 he was appointed cashier of the bank of the United States at Lexington. A service was established in 1838; and by 1843 there was a synagogue which, under the name of "Adas Israel," obtained a charter from the legislature. Louisville now (1901) has six congregations as well as a considerable number of philanthropic and educational institutions. The major **Louisville.** portion of the Jews of Kentucky reside in Louisville; but there are communities in at least a half-dozen other towns in the state.

The remaining Southern states, with a single exception, can be but barely mentioned here. Jews settled in the territory which is now Alabama as early as 1724; and the first congregation was formed in Mobile in 1841. Birmingham, Mobile, Montgomery, and many smaller towns have flourishing communities.

Texas: Jews played a very considerable part in the settlement and development of Texas. The first Jewish settler was Samuel Israel, who came from the United States in 1821, when Texas was still a portion of Mexico. He received a grant of land in Fort Bend county, and later a bounty-warrant in Polk county for services in the army of Texas in 1836 and 1837. He was followed by Abraham C. Labat, of Charleston, S. C., who arrived in 1831. One of the first to take advantage of the new channel of trade opened to the United States by the results of the battle of San Jacinto in 1836, which made Texas an independent republic, was Jacob de Cordova, of Spanish Town, Jamaica. In 1837 he settled in Galveston and became a citizen of the republic; and he had a large share in settling persons on tracts of land in Texas.

The most important of the early settlers, however, was Henry Castro, pioneer of that portion of Texas to the west of the city of San Antonio. **Early** He served in the French army, and **Settlers.** emigrated to the United States after the fall of Napoleon in May, 1827, and, having become an American citizen, was appointed consul for Naples at Providence, R. I. On June 15, 1842, Castro entered into a contract with President Houston for settling a colony west of the Medina. This colony he inaugurated Sept. 3, 1844; and it is estimated that between 1843 and 1846 he introduced more than 5,000 emigrants into the state. On the admission of Texas into the Union, a Jew, David S. Kauffman, was elected one of her congressmen; and he served until his death in 1851. Texas, in proportion to her Jewish population, has had an unusually large number of Jewish citizens prominent in public life and in the learned professions. Thirty-two towns now have Jewish communities; the largest being those of Dallas, Galveston, Houston, San Antonio, and Waco.

Western States.—Indiana: As regards Hebrews in the Western states, the first definite information is of the arrival in Indianapolis in 1794 of Jews from England; but no congregation appears to have been organized there until 1856. This congregation was, however, preceded by those of Fort Wayne (1848), Lafayette (1849), and Evansville (1858). Twenty-three towns in the state now have Jewish communities.

Michigan: A congregation was organized in Detroit, Mich., in 1851. That city now has a considerable Jewish community. In no other place in the state have Jews settled in large numbers. They are, however, distributed in small numbers throughout the whole of Michigan, there being no less than 26 towns with Jewish communities, among which should be especially mentioned Alpena, Bay City, Grand Rapids, and Kalamazoo.

Ohio: The earliest Jewish community of importance in the West, and that which still plays a leading part in Jewish affairs in the United States, is the community of the state of Ohio, more especially that of Cincinnati.

The Jewish pioneer of the Ohio valley was Joseph Jonas, who was born in Exeter, England, and arrived in Cincinnati on March 8, 1817. In 1819 he was joined by three others. Many more, all of English birth, followed, until the year 1830, when a wave of German emigration flowed into Cincinnati. As early as 1819, services were held on New-year's Day and on the Day of Atonement. In 1825 a congregation was formed, under the name "Kahal Kadosh B'ne Yisrael." Two others were established in 1841, and a fourth in 1848. Largely through the influence of Isaac M. Wise, but powerfully aided by capable and public-spirited members of the com- **Cincinnati.** munity, Cincinnati has indelibly impressed itself upon Judaism in America. It is the seat of the Union of American-Hebrew Congregations, of the Board of Delegates, and of the Hebrew Union College, which now supplies the pulpits of a large majority of the Reformed congregations of the United States.

Second in importance is the community of Cleveland, in which Jews settled as early as 1839. A congregation was founded in 1846, and a second in 1850. Jews are now settled in 20 towns in the state.

Illinois: The state of New York contains more than one-third of the Jewish population of the United States; and the states of Pennsylvania and Illinois together comprise one fifth, these two latter being about equal. This is all the more surprising in view of the comparatively recent opening-up of the western territory; though it is quite certain that there were Jewish settlers in the Illinois territory during French rule about 1700.

Chicago received its charter not earlier than the year 1837. The first authentic information of the settlement of Jews there dates back to 1841; and in 1843 a large number arrived. The first Jew to buy land in Cook county was Henry Meyer, who came to Illinois in the spring of 1847. In 1845 the first Jewish organization was established under the name of "The Jewish Burial-Ground Society." The Kehillat Anshe Ma'arab was organized in 1847, being the oldest congregation in the Northwest; a second, B'nai Sholom, was established in 1852. In 1858 the first steps were taken toward the formation of a Jewish Reform association, which resulted in the establishment of the Sinai Congregation in 1861. Since that time the growth of the Jewish community there has been in every way proportionate to the growth of the city itself, which, though not yet 70 years old, is in point of population the second city in the United States. Fifty congregations are known to exist; and there are no doubt many smaller ones whose names have not yet been ascertained. The Jewish community of Chicago has many notable educational establishments and hospitals, and has furnished distinguished members of the legal profession, architects, and musicians. Among its prominent rabbis Liebmann Adler, B. Felsenthal, and Emil G. Hirsch may be named. Jewish communities are known to exist in 16 cities and towns of the state.

Chicago.

Central and Southwestern States: Of these but a bare mention can be made here.

Missouri: For a year previous to the admission of Missouri into the Union as a state, the territory was inhabited by Jews, a family by the name of Bloch having settled there in 1816.

The first religious services were held in St. Louis in 1836, and in 1837 a congregation was established. St. Louis and Kansas City now have very considerable Jewish communities, and smaller ones exist in 8 other towns in the state.

Tennessee: There are Jewish communities in Memphis, Nashville, Knoxville, and other towns.

Minnesota: The first congregation in Minnesota was established at St. Paul in 1856, which now has a considerable community, as has also Minneapolis; Duluth ranking third. Milwaukee has also a large Jewish community, the first congregation having been established in 1852. It has now no less than 5 congregations; and there are congregations in 13 other towns of Wisconsin.

Iowa: The oldest congregation in Iowa is that of Keokuk, founded in 1856. The largest congregation is in Des Moines; and Jews now live in 11 towns in the state, though in small numbers and greatly scattered.

Kansas: The earliest congregation seems to have been that of Leavensworth, founded in 1860. Eight towns now have Jewish communities.

Nebraska: The first Jewish congregation was founded about 1870 in Omaha, which now has a considerable community. There are also congregations at Lincoln and several smaller towns throughout the state.

California: Jews went to the Pacific coast in large numbers on the announcement of the discovery of gold in 1849; and as early as 1850 two congregations had been established in San Francisco. The community grew with great rapidity; and it differed somewhat from the other Jewish communities in the United States at that time, in that while the sole additions of population to the eastern part of the United States were from Germany, California received quotas from England, France, and Holland as well. Sacramento, Los Angeles, and many other towns have congregations; but the bulk of the Jews in the state are in San Francisco. There are at least 11 congregations in this city, a hospital, an orphan asylum, and many other organizations. As a result of this movement toward the Far West, settlements have been made in other states.

Other States and Territories: Jews were in Oregon as early as 1850, and in the city of Portland a congregation was founded in 1858.

At Salt Lake City a congregation was established in 1881; but it is asserted that Jews went there much earlier and furnished a few converts to Mormonism.

Colorado has its principal community in Denver, the earliest congregation there having been established in 1874. A National Home for Consumptives was opened in that city in 1899. There are communities in 7 other towns of the state.

The great wave of Russian immigration has also pushed westward. **Montana, Washington,** and **North and South Dakota** now have congregations. It may be confidently asserted that, in spite of the apparent congestion on the eastern seaboard, there is no state or territory in the Union which at the present writing (1901) is without a Jewish community. Indeed, this statement may be extended to include the distant territories recently brought under the jurisdiction of the United States; since there are already congregations in Porto Rico, in the Hawaiian Islands, and in the Philippines.

Canada: Aaron Hart, born in London, England, 1724, who was in the British army about 1760, seems to have been the first Jewish settler in Canada. In that decade a dozen or more men of means settled in Montreal; and in 1768 they formed a congregation which took the name of "Shearith Israel." In 1807 the question of the political status of the Jew was raised by the election of Ezekiel Hart as a member of the legislature. Refusing to take the oath on the faith of a Christian, he was allowed by the clerk to take it in the Jewish form and with head covered; but, after an exciting debate, his seat was declared vacant and the election null. He was reelected by a heavy majority, but was again prevented from taking his seat; and a bill was brought in to disqualify Jews for seats in the House of Assembly. The governor-general on May 15, 1809, highly displeased with the legislature, dissolved the House; and it was not until 1831 that all the disqualifications of Jews were removed. It is a noteworthy fact that Canada extended full political rights to Jews more than a quarter of a century before the mother-country.

Political Status of Jews.

The first regular minister of the Montreal synagogue was J. R. Cohen, who settled in Montreal about 1778. The most distinguished minister of the congregation was Abraham de Sola, who held office from 1846 to 1882, and was a well-known author and professor of Hebrew in McGill University. A German congregation was established there in 1846, and a Reform congregation in 1882. Since 1890 a large number of Russian Jews have immigrated to Canada, many of whom have engaged in agricultural pursuits. Jews are also settled in Toronto, in Halifax (Nova Scotia), in Victoria, Winnipeg, and in various portions of Manitoba.

Waves of Immigration: All the great nations of historic times have been composed of immigrants. Pressure of population, the nomadic or seafaring spirit, the desire for adventure, for conquest, or for commerce, the tyranny of governments or of churches, have all contributed to turn the human race into a vast migratory species, more capable of adaptability as it is to new environment, than any other form of life. In the birth of intense national feeling following upon the establishment of the German empire, the fact has frequently been lost sight of that none of the peoples now inhabiting any great state is indigenous.

The expulsion of the Jews from Spain, and later from Portugal, and the activity of the Inquisition against the secret Jews, called Maranos, in those countries, coupled with the circumstance that these two peoples were the principal explorers and colonizers of Central and South America, were the factors in determining the early immigration of Jews to America, which was composed exclusively of Spanish and Portuguese exiles, who settled in all the islands to which ships from these countries went. This immigration began with the first settlement of the American continent, and was almost exclusively confined to Central and South America; although the settlers who arrived at Savannah, Ga., in 1733 went direct from Lisbon, making but the briefest stay in England. As the immigration gradually spread in South America small numbers of settlers made their way from Brazil, Curaçao, or the West India Islands to North America, and thence the first Jewish settlements in what is now the United States were derived.

Spanish and Portuguese Exiles.

To Spain and Portugal Holland succeeded as an exploring nation in the early part of the seventeenth century. With the outbreak of the revolt of the Netherlands against Spain in 1567 there developed, by way of protest against the bigotry of the Spaniards, the broadest toleration then known in Europe. By the middle of the century, when Holland had extorted recognition of her independence even from Spain, when she was in league with England and Sweden and was at the height of her power, many Jews of wealth, learning, and influence—largely though not exclusively Spanish exiles—had settled in her dominions; and these were deeply interested in the Dutch West India Company, which determined the attitude of the government toward the settlement of Jews in their new dominions. The Jews in Brazil, moreover, recognizing the favorable attitude of the Holland government toward their coreligionists, powerfully aided the Dutch in their successful attack upon Brazil in 1624. The Dutch dominion lasted until 1654; and during the intervening period many Dutch Jews came to Brazil and other settlements, thus reinforcing the original migration from Spain and Portugal. Owing to the reconquest of Brazil and the subsequent flight of the Jews, these Spanish, Portuguese, and Dutch Jews found their way to the West India Islands and to North America. Jews began to go to New Amsterdam from Holland probably as early as 1652. These, then, constitute the main source whence the Sephardic-Jewish settlers were derived, although stragglers came from France, from England, and even from the Orient, at an early period. It should be stated, however, that not all of the Dutch Jews were of Sephardic stock. Proportionate to the extent of English colonization in the West India Islands surprisingly few Jews went from England to the American colonies or the West India Islands. Some undoubtedly did go to Jamaica and other islands, as well as to the continent, even up to the beginning of the present century; and they were pioneers in several states, but rather as individuals than in any considerable bodies. This is no doubt due to the fact that at the period of the earliest settlement of America there were few if any Jews in England; and later on they were too well satisfied with the conditions there to seek a home elsewhere, although a small number did go to Canada.

Dutch-Sephardic Jews.

Jews of the Ashkenazic rite went early to America, but only as stragglers; an occasional one, to Mexico; and a few, from Holland, to New Amsterdam. From 1730 forward Germany was a theater of war and petty persecutions and of the drafting of able-bodied men into the armies, either for local purposes or to be sold as mercenaries to foreign powers. As the result of a desire to escape these hardships there ensued a steady immigration of Germans to New York, to Georgia, and, above all, to Pennsylvania, where Germans were most hospitably received. In 1750 the German settlers in Pennsylvania alone were estimated at 90,000 out of a total population of 270,000; and among this enormous number there was quite a considerable body of Jews. A lesser number had settled in New York within the same period.

Ashkenazic Jews.

The first partition of Poland in 1772, and the unsettlement of affairs consequent thereupon, brought the first contingent of Polish Jews (through Germany) to America; and this number gradually grew with the successive disasters to Poland and the incorporation of the territory and people with Russia, Germany, and Austria. The Napoleonic wars, the general misery which followed in Germany, the desire to avoid military conscription, the eager wish to partake of the advantages offered in the new country, all impelled a steady stream of German-Jewish immigration to the United States beginning about 1830, reaching its height between 1848 and 1850, and continuing until 1870, when it ceased to be a considerable factor. This immigration was principally from South Germany, from the Rhine provinces, and more especially from Bavaria. The immigrants were mostly from small towns; rarely from the larger cities or from North Germany, which contained well-organized Jewish communities.

German-Jewish Immigration.

The most momentous, and at the same time the most easily recognized wave of immigration was that from Russia, which practically began in 1882. Restrictive measures against the Jews had been for a long time enforced in the empire. The Jews were regarded as a legacy from Poland, and were practically confined to that region; but many had gradually settled in other parts of the empire. In May, 1882, a series of the most proscriptive laws ever passed against Jews in any country was promulgated. These laws practically forbade residence outside of a narrow pale of settlement, restricted higher and secondary education of Jews, mercantile and professional pursuits, and left open no course but emigration en bloc. A small portion of this emigration was directed by Baron de Hirsch to the Argentine Republic, and some to Canada; but the great bulk, by a natural impulse, came to the United States. In the past year (1900) it would appear from available figures that no less than 600,000 Russian-Galician Jews migrated to the United States; and within the year the proscriptive laws of Rumania have started a tide whose force none can foresee. These various movements have given America the third largest Jewish population in the world, and will probably in the future remove the center of Jewish activity to the United States.

Russian Jews.

Education: In the very earliest years of the establishment of the first Jewish congregation in New York city there was attached to the synagogue a school in which ordinary, as well as Hebrew, branches were taught. It was one of the earliest general schools in America. Religious education and instruction in Hebrew were established in connection with most of the early synagogues or were given privately; while for ordinary secular education the Jews resorted to the schools and colleges in existence, although these were largely under the patronage of one or another sect of the Christian church. There was a Jewish matriculate at the University of Pennsylvania, for instance, as early as 1772. As has already been noted, there was established in Philadelphia as early as 1838 a general Sunday-school quite irrespective of congregational organization; and this was the beginning of a movement, which has spread throughout the country, for the organization of educational work along lines quite independent of congregational activities.

Early Jewish Matriculates.

A similar school was organized in Charleston, S. C., in the same year; in the following year, one in Richmond, Va.; in 1845 this movement spread to New York, being taken up first by the Emanuel Society, although the Shearith Israel congregation had started a Hebrew school system as early as 1808. In 1840 MORDECAI M. NOAH, a well-known traveler, politician, and journalist, urged the formation of a Jewish college in the United States; and in 1848 the Hebrew Education Society was founded at Philadelphia—originally a school for general instruction in the ordinary branches up to and through the grade of grammar school, coupled with instruction in Hebrew and in the Jewish religion. In 1864 the Hebrew Free School Association was incorporated in New York; and throughout various states of the Union a movement gradually spread for the organization of free religious schools which would bring into a common school system children from the various congregations in each city. These were largely intended to supersede the private instruction that had theretofore been given. They were, in the main, carried on by volunteer teachers; and their distinguishing feature was that the instruction was usually conducted by native-born persons and in the English language as against the German teaching in the congregational schools.

Organization of Free Schools.

The whole tendency of this educational work was toward the unification of the community and the bringing-out of its individual members from the rather narrow congregational life that had prevailed. Within the last decade or so there has been a decided reaction; and religious schools and Sabbath-schools have been highly organized in connection with individual congregations. Particular stress is laid upon them by the congregations; and much of the communal strength is derived from them. While the Hebrew education societies and schools continue in existence, they do not develop or flourish as might be expected; in fact, since 1882 they have largely taken upon themselves an entirely new function. With the sudden arrival in this country of the large number of Russian Jews having no knowledge of the English language, and in many cases without any particular handicraft, there devolved upon the American Jewish community the necessity of providing, first, day and night schools for teaching the new arrivals English; and, second, manual training and technical schools. These have been established in New York, Philadelphia, Chicago, and in other cities, more or less with the aid of the Baron de Hirsch Fund.

Technical Schools.

Of higher education there has been nothing general, but only special and theological. In 1855 I. M. Wise projected a theological college in Cincinnati under the name of "Zion College"; but the plan came to naught. In 1867 there was established, largely through the instrumentality of Isaac Leeser, Maimonides College at Philadelphia, which, however, was of scarcely longer duration than its predecessor. It was not until the year 1875 that there was founded, by the Union of American Hebrew Congregations, the Hebrew Union College of Cincinnati, which is devoted to the training of rabbis and teachers. While theoretically without partizan bias, it is practically the representative of the Reform wing in America. In 1886 there was established in New York the Jewish Theological Seminary, also for the training of rabbis and teachers, and representing the Orthodox wing of the community. In 1893 there was founded in Philadelphia, through a trust vested in the Mickve Israel congregation by Hyman Gratz, Gratz College, which is devoted to the preparation of teachers for Jewish schools, practically occupying the place of a normal school.

Theological Institutions.

Throughout the United States there have been established in connection with the various congregations, and also independently, societies and Young Men's Hebrew associations which are to a certain extent educational in their character. They usually sustain small libraries and provide lecture-courses on secular and religious topics. In 1893 there was founded the Jewish Chautauqua Society, which has branches all over the country and bears the same relation to the regular schools and colleges as does the University Extension movement, as interpreted in America, to regular colleges for university work. The COUNCIL OF JEWISH WOMEN has engaged to a considerable extent in educational work among its own members. In 1886 there was organized a Sabbath-school Union for the purpose of promoting uniformity and approved methods in Sabbath-school instruction. There are at present (1900) in the United States 415 Jewish educational organizations, 291 of which are religious schools attached to congregations, with 1,127 teachers and an attendance of about 25,000 pupils. There are also 27 Jewish free schools, chiefly in large cities, with about 11,000 pupils and 142 teachers.

Three societies have been organized in the United States to issue Jewish publications—the first, in Philadelphia in 1845; the second, in New York in 1873, and the third, in Philadelphia in 1888. This last is a flourishing organization, and has issued many instructive and important works. Among the educational activities should also be mentioned the American Jewish Historical Society organized in 1892. Associated with many of the schools there are now circulating and reference libraries, as well as several independent ones, the largest of which is the Aguilar Library in New York, founded in 1886. The Maimonides Library of the Independent Order B'ne B'rith in New York was organized in 1851.

Publication Societies and Libraries.

It should be said in this connection that this Order and many of the other Orders and lodges had educational features—lectures and otherwise—and did pioneer work in the education of their members.

Of Jewish periodicals and newspapers published at one time or another in the United States, not less than 83 have been in English or German, 16 in Hebrew, and 82 in Yiddish.

Philanthropy: Of the philanthropic work of Jews in America practically nothing is known outside of the United States and Canada; and under these heads the subject will be treated in detail. In a general way it may be said that, until a very recent time, philanthropic work took the form of ordinary charity. The poor were clothed, fed, and kept warm, the sick were visited, and the dead were buried. The higher philanthropic work, that of preventing poverty by improvement of conditions and surroundings, is but a recent development. From the earliest arrival of Jews in this country, it was their ideal that none of their poor should become a charge upon the general community; and in the earlier days charity was dispensed by individuals, or by funds collected through the congregations; the former, however, being the prevalent means.

Early Individual Charity.

A well-to-do family, or even one in but comfortable circumstances, would care for one or more poorer families, supplying them regularly with the necessaries of life. Gradually, as the Hebrew population increased, this method proved to be inadequate, and societies—generally small, and having specific objects—were formed. Some were for the visitation of the sick and the burial of the dead; some, in connection with congregations, for general charitable purposes; and some for the distribution of unleavened bread for the Passover. Still later, as the need grew, associations for the care of orphans, hospitals for the care of the sick, and, later still, homes for the aged were erected. Most of these societies and institutions were small; their work was done with insufficient funds and by voluntary officers, and without a definite plan. It was seen that this scattering of forces produced waste, and it was feared that it tended to pauperism; so that in all the large cities a gradual amalgamation took place of the various charitable organizations into one society with a trained officer. These societies usually included all the organizations, with the exception of the hospitals and the orphan asylums, in a given city, and had for their purpose the rendering of immediate relief. Later still, in each of a few cities, a central organization was formed, which included the hospitals and orphan asylums, and whose object it was to have a central body to collect funds for all the charitable organizations in the city and to distribute them pro rata. Of recent years it has been realized that this highly organized method of distributing charity has resulted in placing the whole matter on a somewhat mechanical basis, and has not always been productive of such good results as the old and unscientific giving from man to man, which bore with it the evidence of a certain human sympathy. Consequently in all the large cities an endeavor is being made to return to a more personal relation between the rich and the poor; and Sisterhoods or Personal Service societies have been organized to aid in the intelligent and sympathetic distribution of relief.

Charitable Organizations.

The most recent development has been the National Conference of Jewish Charities in the United States, founded Dec. 1, 1899, in Cincinnati, and composed of 40 relief organizations. Its object is to promote reforms in administration and uniformity of action without interfering with the work of any local society. There are at present 15 homes for orphans, or societies for their care, in the United States; 12 homes for the aged; and 9 hospitals. It is estimated that there are 593 Jewish philanthropic organizations in the United States.

Philanthropic Homes.

Religious Development: Until a very recent date, religious development was not marked by any special feature. The Jews who came to the Spanish and Portuguese settlements were all Maranos who, while attached to the Catholic Church at home, had secretly observed the tenets of their own religion, and had, to a certain extent, mingled the rites of Catholicism with those of their own faith. From the testimony given in Inquisition trials it appears that quite a series of new customs arose from this mixture.

In the Dutch settlements, the Dutch tradition was usually maintained, the rabbis being imported from Amsterdam. From the very beginning the Jews in the United States consisted of both Sephardim and Ashkenazim; but the former were at first in the majority, and organized the four earliest congregations in the country; namely, those of New York, Newport, Savannah, and Philadelphia. As early as 1766 a translation into English of the Prayers—probably the first English-Jewish Prayer-Book ever issued—was published in New York.

In Jamaica and in Canada there has always been more or less direct relation with England; but in the United States the entire religious life of Jews has been especially characterized by the absence of dependence upon any European authority, as well as by the absence of any central authority in America. Congregational autonomy has been the watchword.

Reform Movement Begun in Charleston.

The movement for ceremonial reform began in Charleston in 1825. It was strongly supported in Albany, and later in Cincinnati, by I. M. Wise, from 1850, but did not make much headway until the arrival in the United States of David Einhorn and Samuel Hirsch. Under the influence of these men and of other rabbis,—principally from Germany—the trend toward alterations in the liturgy and ritual set in very strongly; but about 1880 a reaction against the radical tendencies took place, even on the part of some congregations professedly attached to the Reform movement, resulting in the formation of an intermediate or a Conservative group. With the influx of large numbers of Russian Jews, many congregations of the Orthodox type were established. The general attitude of Jews in America is one of very considerable attachment to the principles of their religion coupled with a gradual abandonment of many of the forms and ceremonies, although apostasy and actual defections from the synagogue are rare (see AMERICA, JUDAISM IN).

Services to the State in Military and in Civil Life: As has already been pointed out under "Brazil," the Jews rendered great service to the Dutch in their conquest of Brazil in 1624 and afterward in 1646-54 against the Portuguese. They also made a brave resistance against the French fleets which attacked Surinam in 1689 and 1712 respectively, and played a considerable part in the suppression of negro revolts in the same country between 1690 and 1772. They had a separate company of which David Nassy was captain, and, later, Isaac Carvalho (1743).

Earliest Jewish Settlers Were Soldiers.

The first Jewish settlers in Canada were soldiers who came over in Braddock's army, and there is record of their being engaged later on in encounters with the Indians. There were one or two Jews in Washington's expedition across the Alleghanies in 1754. When the first agitation began which ended in the Revolutionary War, the Jews, like their fellow citizens, were divided. Some remained loyal to the British crown; but the great majority adhered to the Patriot cause. There were 9 Jewish signers to the "non-importation" resolutions of 1763; and when the war actually broke out, they not only risked their lives, but some, like Haym Solomon, helped with their money to equip and maintain the armies of the Revolution.

So far, the names of 45 Jews who served as officers and privates in the continental armies have been put on record; and this can hardly be the total number, as a considerable proportion were officers. Possibly the best known of the latter was David S. Franks, who was major, and afterward lieutenant-colonel, on the staff of General Arnold. In the war of 1812 there were, as far as known, 43 Jews, of whom the most prominent was Brigadier-General Joseph Bloomfield, in charge of Military District No. 4, comprising Pennsylvania, Delaware, and western New Jersey. In the Mexican War there were 57 Jews, the most prominent being David de Leon, who twice received the thanks of Congress for gallantry. In the Civil War there were on both sides 7,038 Jewish soldiers, and in the Spanish-American War over 2,000. Besides, a fair number has been found in the regular army, as well as in the navy (see ARMY, JEWS IN, and UNITED STATES).

In civil service to the state nearly all of the information at hand relates to the United States. There **Services in Civil Life.** have been 4 Jewish members of the United States Senate and about 20 of the House of Representatives. Many have been in the diplomatic and consular services, among whom may be specially mentioned Mordecai M. Noah, consul at Tunis; B. F. Peixotto, consul at Bucharest; Simon Wolf, consul-general in Egypt; Oscar S. Straus, twice minister to Turkey, and Solomon Hirsch, who held the same post.

Jews have served as mayors of cities, members of the legislature, judges of the courts; and they have held many minor offices of trust and confidence. Simon W. Rosendale was attorney-general of New York; Isador Raynor, attorney-general of Maryland.

The first statue to belong to the United States, and which originated Statuary Hall in the Capitol at Washington, was one in bronze of Thomas Jefferson by David d'Angers, a French sculptor. It was presented to the United States in 1838 by a Jew, Lieutenant, afterward Commodore, Uriah P. Levy, of the United States navy, and was formally accepted by Congress in 1874 on the motion of Senator Sumner.

Civil and Political Rights: In the colonies established on American soil more liberty or toleration was usually shown to the Jews than in the mother countries, yet they labored under serious disabilities. In Lima, in Peru, and in Mexico they were sued by the Inquisition. In the Dutch West Islands and provinces they were accorded the t freedom. In New Amsterdam, while there was some objection to them, and they ng were at first denied burghers' rights, the latter seem to have been granted them at a very early date—a result due largely, as already stated, to the persistence, both by petitions and before the courts, of Asser Levy. In 1685, Jews were formally granted the exercise of their religion. The British ent in 1753 passed an act permitting "professing the Jewish religion to be naturalized rliament," which was repealed in the following ear. Not until 1858 might Jews sit in Parliament; and it was only in 1860 that the words "on true faith of a Christian" were removed from ordinary oath.

he English provincial governors and assemblies ibited a tolerant spirit much earlier. Dr. Lumbrozo was granted letters of denization in Maryland early as Sept. 10, 1663. In 1670 Sir Thomas Lynch, governor of Jamaica, was instructed to give all possible encouragement to persons of differing sions. In 1672 Rabba Couty of New York appealed to the king in council, and promptly obtained redress for a grievance. In 1674 in Barbados Jews were allowed to take the oath upon the five books of Moses. A law passed in Jamaica in 1683 required applicants for naturalization simply to take the oath of allegiance. In 1727 the General Assembly of New York voted that Jews taking the oath of abjuration might omit the words "upon the true faith of a Christian."

This liberality was not confined, however, to provincial assemblies. In 1740 Parliament passed an **In the British Colonies.** act for naturalizing, among others, such Jews "as are settled or shall settle in any of His Majesty's colonies in America." Of the 189 Jews who took advantage of this act, 151 were in Jamaica, 24 in New York, 9 in Pennsylvania, 4 in Maryland, and 1 in South Carolina. Following the Declaration of Independence in 1776 most of the states placed all citizens upon an absolute equality; the only notable exception being Maryland, in which state a prolonged struggle took place before full political rights were finally secured (see above, under "Maryland").

The stringent Sunday laws now in force in nearly all the states, forbidding Jews to work on the Christian Sunday, entail considerable hardship among Jews observing the Sabbath; but these laws are in the nature of police regulations, and are not discriminative against Jews as such.

Science and Art, Literature, and the Learned Professions: Jews have been members of all the learned professions—principally the legal and medical—and they have contributed to nearly all the sciences and to the fine arts. The fact has already been mentioned that some Jews have been elevated to the bench, and others elected to the post of attorney-general. Many eminent physicians, medical writers, and professors in medical schools are Jews. There has been at least one distinguished Hebrew sculptor, Moses Ezekiel, and there are several others of rank. Among artists and etchers **Jews Eminent in All Departments.** should especially be mentioned the Rosenthals of Philadelphia, father and son; and of illustrators the best known is Louis Loeb. Jews are also found as inventors, e.g., Emil Berliner, inventor of the telephone transmitter; as architects, Dankmar Adler of Chicago, and Arnold W. Brunner of New York, for instance; and as engineers, the most distinguished of whom is Mendes Cohen of Baltimore, one of the pioneer railroad builders of the country, and at one time president of the American Society of Civil Engineers.

Many Jews hold professorships in colleges: M. Bloomfield and J. H. Hollander at Johns Hopkins; Richard Gottheil and E. R. A. Seligman at Columbia; Morris Loeb at the University of New York; Morris Jastrow at the University of Pennsylvania; Joseph Jastrow at the University of Wisconsin; Charles Gross at Harvard; while a much larger number are assistant professors or instructors.

The most distinguished Jewish writer of poetry in the United States was Emma Lazarus; Michael Heilprin gained eminence as an editor and writer; A. Cahan and Emma Wolf are successful novelists; and Morris Rosenfeld is a gifted Yiddish poet.

In music a number of Hebrews have acquired a reputable position. Jews are also prominent as actors and as dramatic authors. Among the latter **Music and the Stage.** may be mentioned Aaron J. Phillips, who first appeared in New York at the Park Theater in 1815 and was a very successful comedian; Emanuel Judah, who first appeared in 1823; and Moses S. Phillips, who acted at the Park Theater in 1827. Mordecai M. Noah, best known as journalist, politician, and diplomat, was also a dramatic author of considerable note. Other dramatists and authors were Samuel B. H. Judah (born in New York in 1790) and Jonas B. Phillips; and at the present time David Belasco is a most successful playwright. It would be impossible to enumerate the Jews now on the stage. The introduction of opera into the United States was due largely to the instrumentality of Jews.

In Commerce and Manufacture: In commerce Jews were notably important in the eighteenth century. The fact that the earliest settlers were men of means, and were Spanish and Portuguese Jews who had relatives and friends settled throughout the Levant, gave them specially favorable opportunities for trading. Some were ship-owners; one man, Aaron Lopez of Newport, had before the Revolutionary War a fleet of thirty vessels. Jews very early traded between the West India Islands and the North American colonies, as well as with Amsterdam, Venice, etc.

The Jewish immigrants who arrived in America during the nineteenth century were in the main poor people who commenced trading in a small way, usually by peddling, which, before the existence of railroads, was a favorite method of carrying merchandise into the country districts. By industry and frugality they laid the foundations of a considerable number of moderate fortunes. The Jews in New York became an integral part of that great trading community.

In the early colonial period, more especially in Pennsylvania and in New York, many of the Jews traded with the Indians.

The organization under which the Stock Exchange of New York was formed, originated in an agreement in 1792 to buy or sell only on a definite commission; and to this document were attached the signatures of four Jews. Since then Jews have

Jews Active in Financial Circles. been very active in the Stock Exchange and in banking circles, both in New York and elsewhere. They have also taken a leading part in controlling the cotton trade. Jews are likewise very prominent in the manufacture of cloaks and shirts in the clothing trade, and more recently in cigars and jewelry.

In 1888 Markens estimated that the wholesale trade in the hands of Jews in the city of New York amounted to $248,000,000, and the holdings of real estate to $150,000,000.

Agriculture: Jews were the first to introduce the culture of the sugar-cane on the western continent and of the vine in Georgia. Otherwise their agricultural activity was extremely limited until the arrival of Russian Jews, from 1881 forward, and the powerful impulse given through them to agriculture by emigration societies, by the Baron de Hirsch Fund, and by their own great desire to revert to the cultivation of the soil (see AGRICULTURAL COLONIES IN THE UNITED STATES).

Social: The social organization of the Jews resident in America has differed little from that in other countries. In the early colonial period the wealthier Hebrews seem to have taken part with their Christian fellow citizens in the organization of dances and other social functions, and clubs; and it is a matter of record that the wealthier Jewish families lived with comparative good taste and possessed fine houses, objects of art, etc. Nevertheless, in the main, and without any compulsion, Jews preferred to live in close proximity to each other.

At the time when little toleration was shown in other countries, there were in America many interchanges of mutual good-will between Christians and Jews. Rabbi Haym Isaac Karigel was apparently a close friend of Ezra Stiles, president of Yale College.

Jews and Christians Cooperate. Gershom Mendes Seixas, minister of the Shearith Israel congregation, New York, was a trustee of Columbia College (1784–1815) although this organization was under the Episcopal Church; and the Episcopal bishop of New York occasionally attended service in the synagogue. After 1848 there arrived a large number of Jews who could not speak the English language, and to them a certain odium attached on this account; but this seems to have gradually worn off. The general American public exhibited great sympathy with the Jews in 1840 at the time of the Damascus murders, and again in 1882 on the occasion of the persecutions in Russia; and Hermann Ahlwardt, on his visit to America in 1895, found the soil an unfavorable one for his anti-Semitic propaganda.

The only indication of any prejudice against the Jews—shown mainly in the Eastern states—has been the exclusion of Jewish children from certain private schools and of Jews generally from some hotels.

Very early the Jews in America began to form social organizations. A club was started in Newport as early as 1769; and social clubs—some comprising

Hebrew Clubs. many members and possessed of magnificent properties—have been established in many sections of the country. This development of Hebrew social clubs has been larger in the United States than anywhere else. American Jews have also been especially given to the forming of secret "Orders," which, while they had primarily an educational and charitable purpose, had much social influence, and tended powerfully toward the continued association of Jews with each other when the hold of the synagogue upon them relaxed. These were supplemented later by the formation of Young Men's Hebrew Associations, which, like the Orders, partook to some extent of the nature of social organizations.

Statistics: In 1818 Mordecai M. Noah estimated the Jewish population of the United States at 3,000 and in 1826 Isaac C. Harby set it at 6,000. In the "American Almanac" gave the number 000; and in 1848 M. A. Berk estimated it at The first systematic attempt to obtain st information was undertaken by the Board gates of American Israelites, through a com which William B. Hackenburg, Si others were members. They estim population in 1880 at 230,257. In 18 estimated it at 400,000.

In the reports on the statistics of United States at the eleventh census Jewish statistics were collected by Philip His investigations showed that there were 5 gregations with 130,496 communicants. Of congregations, 301 worshiped in edifices with a proximate seating capacity of 139,284. cupied 232 halls and rooms, having an aggre seating capacity of 28,477. The total value of synagogue property was estimated at $9,754,95

In 1897 David Sulzberger estimated the total p ulation at 937,800; and in 1905 it was estimated 1,253,213.

CYRUS ADLER.